The Dear Collection

The Bear Collection

Story told by David Caddy
Illustrations by Chantal Stewart

To my grandfathers

The Bear Collection

Text: David Caddy
Editors: Brigid James, Writers Reign
Design: design rescue
Illustrations: Chantal Stewart
Typeset in: Plantin

PM Library
Ruby Level B
Supernova!
Firelight Secrets
The Bear Collection
Hop to It, Minty!
The Big Toe Robbery
Ben's Tune

Text © 2001 Cengage Learning Australia Pty Limited
Illustrations © 2001 Cengage Learning Australia Pty Limited

ALL RIGHTS RESERVED. No part of this work covered
by the copyright herein may be reproduced, transmitted,
stored or used in any form or by any means graphic,
electronic, or mechanical, including but not limited to
photocopying, recording, scanning, digitising, taping,
Web distribution, information networks, or information
storage and retrieval systems, except as permitted by
the Australian Copyright Act 1968, without the prior
written permission of the publisher.

ISBN 978 1 86 961468 3
ISBN 978 1 86 961465 2 (set)

Cengage Learning Australia
Level 7, 80 Dorcas Street
South Melbourne, Victoria Australia 3205
Phone: 1300 790 853

Cengage Learning New Zealand
Unit 4B Rosedale Office Park
331 Rosedale Road, Albany, North Shore NZ 0632
Phone: 0508 635 766

For learning solutions, visit cengage.com.au

Printed in China by 1010 Printing International Ltd
18 19 20 21 15 14 13

Contents

Chapter 1	The Lost Bear	6
Chapter 2	The Antique Shop	9
Chapter 3	Jim Finds a Bear	12
Chapter 4	Mr Tucker Is Annoyed	15
Chapter 5	Jim Is Worried	19
Chapter 6	Zelda Buys a Bear	24
Chapter 7	Grandpa's Visit	27
	A Note About Teddy Bears	31

Chapter 1

The Lost Bear

Jim had only twenty-four hours to find all the bears before Grandpa arrived. Many of Jim's antique bears had been part of Grandpa's own collection and he had helped Jim collect more. Grandpa would want to see all the old bears lined up when he came to visit.

The miniature teddy was under Jim's pillow. The English teddy was behind the curtain. The 1920s black bear was in the wardrobe.

But where were the gold plush bear and the handmade German bear? They were the oldest and best in Jim's collection. Grandpa had said that any collector would be proud to own them.

Jim grabbed his bookcase and pulled it forwards. Books tumbled to the floor. But there, under the bottom shelf, was the gold plush bear. Jim gently picked the bear up, placed it with the others and continued his search for Scraps, the German bear.

Jim's toys, half his clothes, his pillow, his bedcovers and his shoes were soon all over the floor. His collections of stamps, books and coins were upturned.

"What are you doing?" his mother asked, peering around the door. "Have you lost something again?"

Jim sank onto his bed. "I can't find Scraps," he moaned.

"I saw a bear just like him today at the antique shop," Mum said. "I don't suppose it's him?" she joked.

Jim frowned.

"Don't worry!" said Mum. "You've just misplaced him. He's probably somewhere in this mess."

Jim's face felt hot with guilt.

Chapter 2

The Antique Shop

Jim wasn't supposed to take his bears out of the house, but sometimes he did. He remembered carrying Scraps in his backpack. Maybe poor old Scraps had dropped out!

As Jim crawled under his bed, he thought about the antique shop. As he pulled out his sock drawer, and all his socks fell out, he thought about the antique shop. It would close at five o'clock and it was nearly five now.

"I'll be back in ten minutes, Mum! I'm going to the shops," he called.

Jim lived across the road from a grocery store, a bookshop, a computer shop, and an antique shop.

Until last year, Mrs Lamb had owned the antique shop. Jim used to help her unpack boxes of dusty books and old plates. He'd loved helping Mrs Lamb polish the old furniture and look for little treasures in the boxes of junk. Mrs Lamb even used to pay him a small amount, and sometimes she had given him an old coin or a book for his collections.

"You're a born collector, Jim," she used to say with a smile.

Jim felt sad when he thought about her. He missed Mrs Lamb.

When she died, Mr Tucker took over the shop. He didn't like kids, and even though it was the same shop, with the same kinds of things, it even smelled different.

Chapter 3

Jim Finds a Bear

Jim hesitated before entering the shop.

"What are you doing, Jim?" came a voice from behind him.

He turned and saw Zelda Hooper. Her dad owned the computer shop.

Jim didn't answer. He didn't like Zelda.

"What are you doing?" she asked again.

"Nothing," he answered. "I'll see you tomorrow at school!"

"Are you going in there?" she pointed. "It smells!"

"It's just dusty," Jim answered, walking past her. Zelda hurried after him.

The old door swung open, and the tiny bell, which hung from the frame, tinkled. Jim scanned the shop until he saw the bear, high on a shelf. It was Scraps — it had to be! It certainly looked the same.

Zelda's eyes followed his. "Oh yuck, what a *disgusting* old bear!" she sneered.

"It's mine," said Jim.

"How old are you?" Zelda laughed. "Wait till I tell the other kids at school."

Jim knew it was a mistake to tell Zelda what had happened, but if he didn't get his bear back, somebody else might buy it. "Zelda…" he hesitated. "I'm an arctophile, a bear collector. But I've lost one of my bears. I think that's it."

"You mean that old bear, with a seventy-five dollar price tag, is yours!"

"It's a Steiff Zotty teddy bear, made in Germany. It should be three hundred dollars, Zelda. Mrs Lamb would have checked out the price in a catalogue first, but Mr Tucker didn't," he whispered.

"Wow!" exclaimed Zelda.

Chapter 4

Mr Tucker Is Annoyed

A figure came towards them from the shadows at the back of the shop. It was Mr Tucker.

"Mr Tucker," Jim began, in his politest voice.

"I'm closing now," he interrupted. "Out you go!"

"Mr Tucker, I've lost my bear and I think that's it," continued Jim. "Can I have it back?"

"I don't give things away. I'd go broke!" Mr Tucker said crossly.

Jim stared up at the bear and remembered. "He's got his name on a tag pinned to his back," he shouted excitedly. "His name is Scraps, and my name is on the tag, too."

Mr Tucker's eyes closed for what seemed like a year. "If your name's there, you can have it," he grumbled, shuffling over to the bear.

He took the bear down, turned it over and ran his hands around it, but there was no tag.

"Can I look?" asked Jim.

Mr Tucker handed him the bear, and watched as Jim's face dropped.

"Go on, off you go," he ordered.

Outside, Zelda teased him. "It wasn't even yours. Wait until everyone at school hears about this!"

"It is mine," answered Jim. "I'm sure it's mine. Just because the identification tag has fallen off it doesn't mean it isn't mine. It *is* my bear, Zelda, and I've got to get it back by tomorrow."

"That old man probably took the tag off. He just wants to sell it," Zelda accused. "Why don't you just take it?"

"What?" Jim's mouth dropped open.

"If it's yours, then you aren't stealing. You are just taking back what belongs to you."

"Well," Jim hesitated.

"You can't do any harm getting back what is yours," Zelda insisted.

Jim knew Zelda was wrong. Every action has its consequences. If he took the bear without paying, the police could come to his house. Mr Tucker would be very angry and his parents and grandfather would be so disappointed with him.

"Jim! Time to come home," his mother called from their front door.

"Coming, Mum!" he shouted, turning quickly to go.

"I'll see you tomorrow, Jim," Zelda said, with a smirk on her face.

"Yes! I guess you will." Jim forced himself to smile at her.

Chapter 5

Jim Is Worried

As the clock struck midnight, Jim punched his pillow again. How could he get his bear? If he had a month he might be able to raise seventy-five dollars. He could sell all his collections, do extra chores around the house and save his pocket money. But not before his grandfather arrived tomorrow.

Maybe he could work for Mr Tucker and get paid in advance. The shop would smell so much nicer, too, if they polished the furniture. He'd ask Mr Tucker in the morning.

On his way to school, Jim stopped outside the antique shop. It was closed, but he could still see the bear. "Please don't let anyone buy my bear while I'm at school today," he said to himself.

When Jim arrived at school, he saw a small group of children huddled with Zelda. They were laughing and looking in his direction. Zelda, who was often alone, was suddenly popular.

Grant Turnbull caught up with Jim on the way to class. "You don't really still play with teddy bears, do you?" he asked.

By lunchtime, Jim was tired of having to explain about his antique bears. Some kids listened, some kids teased him and some kids didn't care. And all the time he kept thinking that someone might be buying his bear at that very moment.

After school, Jim raced to the antique shop and peered through the window. An old man and his granddaughter were handling his bear. He had to go in!

"Jim!"

He turned. His mother had come to look for him. He looked at his mother. He looked at the shop.

"Jim!" Mum said again.

Jim pressed his face against the glass. The old man was examining his bear. What could he do?

"Listen to me!" Mum sounded cross.

He turned to her again.

"What's wrong with you, Jim? You heard me calling," she scolded. "I need you to get me some things from the grocery store for dinner. You know Grandpa will be here any minute."

"But I just want to go into the antique shop for a while."

"I need these things straight away, so get them first. Then you can go back to the antique shop later," she said.

"But Mum!"

"No arguments! Here's the list and the money."

Chapter 6

Zelda Buys a Bear

Jim dropped his backpack at home and ran to get the groceries. The old man and his granddaughter came out of the antique shop. They hadn't bought anything.

Jim grinned with relief.

He checked that his bear was still in the shop and then bought the groceries for his mother.

On his way home he saw Zelda going into the antique shop. What was she doing? Surely she wasn't going to steal his antique bear? She was the richest kid in his class. But she had talked about stealing it!

Jim turned. He had to stop her. But it was too late. As he reached the shop, she came out, carrying his bear.

"Zelda! You haven't stolen it, have you?" he asked.

"Of course not! I bought it," she answered.

Jim almost hugged her. "Zelda! You're the best. I'll pay you back, I promise."

"You don't think I bought it for you!" she laughed. "Don't be silly. It's mine now. I bought it for seventy-five dollars, and I'm going to sell it for three hundred."

"What?" Jim was confused. "But it's my bear, Zelda!"

Zelda turned and skipped towards her dad's computer shop, tossing the bear into the air and catching it by the leg.

"It's my bear," repeated Jim, taking a step towards her. "Please give it to me!"

Zelda spun around, whipped open the door and ran into her dad's shop.

Chapter 7

Grandpa's Visit

An hour later, Jim was lying on his bed with his face in the pillow. His grandfather came into the room.

"What's the problem, Jim?"

Jim sat up and faced him. He forced out the words. "I'm sorry, but I've lost Scraps, the Steiff Zotty you gave me."

"You couldn't have," Grandpa said gently. "You always hide your bears so well."

He looked around Jim's floor, still covered in toys and clothes. He picked up a large tin box and prised it open. He reached in and withdrew a tray of medals. He grinned. "You haven't lost Scraps. He's still here from last time, remember? Guarding my medals!"

There, well-hidden in the bottom of the tin, was Scraps!

Jim's mum was in the doorway.

"I thought I'd lost him and he was the one in the antique shop," said Jim.

"No!" answered Mum. "I had a good look at that bear today. It's not a handmade Steiff. It's an imitation, not even worth ten dollars."

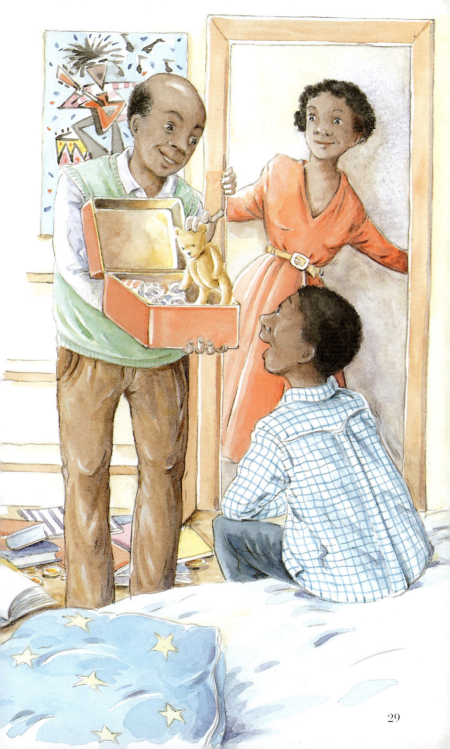

A Note About Teddy Bears

In 1902, President Theodore 'Teddy' Roosevelt was on a hunting trip in Mississippi, when some of his party tracked down a bear and tied it to a tree. When the President arrived at the scene, he would not shoot the bear and ordered that it be set free.

Soon after, a cartoonist captured this moment in a drawing for a newspaper. A New York storekeeper and his wife saw the cartoon, and they decided to stitch a bear by hand. They called it 'Teddy's bear'.

Toymakers around the world copied this idea and the soft toy bear soon came to be known as the teddy bear.

Today collectors of teddy bears are called 'arctophiles' and a collection of teddy bears is called a 'hug'. There are hundreds of thousands of arctophiles around the world.

Teddy bears will qualify as 'real' antiques in 2002, when they will be 100 years old.